ACKNOWLEDGEMENT

Photo of the author credit: Adam Underwood

Editing: Liberty Arbogast , Brian Carleton and Stephen Stewart

Boneless Caviar

Leigh McDowell

Presentation by *BookLeaf Publishing*

Web: www.bookleafpub.com

E-mail: info@bookleafpub.com

ISBN: 9789395621069

First edition 2022

DEDICATION

For my mother, Cinthia - For always doing everything she could with what she had. I wouldn't have traded our life for anything.

For my children: Liberty, Harper and Carter - for being the best parts of my entire existence. I couldn't have wished for better, funnier or more resilient kids. I love each of you so much and I hope you never forget that.

For my best friend and inspiration: Stephen "Nemo" Stewart... for never giving up on me. Thank you. Thank you a million times!

For my person: Adam Underwood, for being my muse at times and actually amusing, the rest of the time.

A Bullet Shaped Like A Child

I Was Waging War Against Myself
You. A Soldier, Too Young To Recruit

But You Were Strong, So I Cast Giant Weapons
In Your Tiny Hands.

"We're The Good Guys, Right Mommy?"
I Shake You. I Break You.

" Who Gives A Fuck Soldier? Now Lace Up
Your Boots! Reach Into Your Pockets, Draw
Your Anger And Shoot!"

I Hug You.
"I'm Sorry, Baby. Soon This All Will Be Over"
Let The Smoke Clear, We Watch The Ashes
Smolder.

I Taught You My Battle Songs-
Hatred-Insanity-Broken Dreams-Struggle

I Forged Your Tongue To A Sharp,
 Deadly Dagger
Wielding My Hammer,
Heavily Clad In False Hope.

I Taught You To Go For The Throat

I Convinced Myself I Was Not Hurting You
Slowly Stripping Color From Your Sight.
I Needed You To See BLACK and WHITE

I Inhaled Smoke That Tasted Of Courage And
Bravery.
Perfectly Disguised With Evil Artificial
Flavoring.

The High Gave Me A False Sense Of Pride.
Something I Pretended Came From Gas Station
Glass Pipes.

-Trading Your Butterfly Kisses For Tear Gas-
-Coloring Books For Blueprints Of The Enemies
Castles-
Battle Plans Drawn Over Traced ABC Ghosts.

 Echoes Of Laughter
 Of The After School Snacker.
This Monument I Should Have Fought Harder
For!
-THE REFRIGERATOR DOOR-
I Remember This Place, Before The War
          I Cry As I Touch It
"Fuck This Kangaroo.
 'I Love You', Bullshit, Mom!
You Taught Me The Art Of War!"

-Pull The Pin-
A Grenade Ricochets
Shrapnel Of Hurt And Neglect.
You Scream Out To The Victims
-Demanding-
"Who's Next?!"
I Question How This All Went Wrong
        I'm So Sorry I Did This To You.
        " It's Ok Mom-
 If This Is The Only Game You Like Playing ,I'll
Play It Just So I'm Playing Something With
You"

Smoke Some More, Find Some Happiness
It Only Hurts A Short While
With My Dying Breath
And Final Thoughts, I Recall Your Sweet Smile.
The Warm Blood, The Exit Wound.
I Feel Your Hug, Somehow Different
Now You Squeeze So I'll Die Soon.
Your Eyes, Once Soft With Kindness
 Stare Off Into The Distance, As I Count Them
For Miles.
-The Drums Beat and The Rifle Fires-
-I Hear War Songs-
- You Play Them-
You're A Bullet Shaped Like My Child.

Leigh McDowell

To My Children

Destinations

IN YOUR EYES I SAW GLIMPSES
 OF WHITE PICKET FENCES

YOUR CHEST FELT LIKE HOME TO ME

YOUR BONES ON MY BONES
CRUSHED ALL MY DEFENSES

YOUR LIPS TASTED LIKE EVERYTHING
I IMAGINED "FOREVER" TO BE

YOUR FINGERTIPS OUTLINED TRACES
 DRAWN ON THE EDGE OF MY SKIN,

MAPS OF ALL THE PLACES
YOU'D TAKE ME THAT I'D NEVER BEEN

NOW YOUR EYES GAZE AND THEY SHIFT
YOUR CHEST CAVES AND IT DIPS
YOUR BONES JUST MOVE MY HIPS
AND YOUR LIPS… I JUST MISS

YOUR FINGERTIPS NOW DRAW LINES,
WHAT'S YOURS AND WHAT'S MINE
MY JAGGED EDGES,

TORN, TATTERED
POSTCARDS TO LOST DESTINATIONS,
 STAMPED "LOVE, ALWAYS!", THE LIES
SCATTERED.

SIGNED: FOREVER YOURS,
             I NEVER MATTERED
LM 2021

The Devil Is A Door To Door Salesman

The devil's eyes are blue too
And he knows just what to say
But beneath nice three piece suits,
New suspenders and boots,
He's just a sales pitch with a name .

You want to know why I won't buy my own
Shame, anymore?

Time and time again
 I gave in to fake salesman
That couldn't give up going
door to door.

I let them sell me like art
Makeshift parts of my heart
Until I didn't own me , anymore.

They told me I was angelic,
loved to dress me up in all blue.
Then tossed me out like a relic;
For something shiny and new.

-what do I do
After being left, now feeling used?

Survival of The Queen

I gathered up the pawns, king and bishops
Never again, I swore..
The last things left to pick up
Were the tired, heavy, worn pieces
Of me - the Queen
off the floor.

No, it wasn't the fighting-
Screaming, scratching or biting
It was loving so damn hard
That made me sore.
And you ask why a girl like me carries a sword?

I learned survival
By being thrown to a den full of lions,
I forced myself to stop crying-
And gathered my tissues in piles-
To make a place to sleep when I got tired.

But my bed was meant to be shared by two.

Do you know what I'd do
Just to have someone I could lie next to
That wouldn't just lie the same way they all do?

I'd take out my pliers
God, I hate liars;
And pull out his lies tooth for tooth.

I know even then I wouldn't get the whole truth.

It's the same sad song on repeat
I've listened to enough of my own heart beat;
I just want to hear to something new.
But If you can't sing along, then what's the use?

Ammo

There may be an X carved into my chest
but I'm not the treasure you mistake me for.

I've become good a pleasure,
so for good measure you'll still find guards
outside my door.

What for?

Oh, that's just the room
where my ammo is stored.

Not to be rude
but I've met monsters
Like you
disguised as men, before.

One Liners

Read on and be inspired,
Lost your voice?
 I'm sure that you can find yours
Inside this book of one liners
That I bought from a liar.
He sold me his love like an island.

But he'd played me for a fool.
Because secretly he'd leased it
In small, tiny pieces
to a number of others, too.

Ship Wrecks and Dragons

He was an honest man,

that he swore.

I lost myself there on that shore.

I was so goddamned sure-

He wasn't collecting the scraps

In between waves as they crashed

Picking up parts, filled with cracks-

from another ship's wreckage

As they all washed ashore.

Do you still wonder what dragons breathe fire
for?

Friendly Fire

He may not have been violent

But he was a pirate

He never loved me

He just loved conquering things he adored.

He took the map of what was left of me

And set fire to the rest of me

You can still smell the ash-

See the scars on each edge of me ,

where he tore.

You see the cannons, all aimed at my door?

Superman's Board Game

I won't throw my white flags out,
I'll just put my walls up;
Think I'll paint these in a pattern
Black and white-
Checker board.
So, continue your quest
There's no "S" on your chest
I'm no damsel in distress -
So what the hell would I need a hero for?

If you still believe you know best
Let's put it to the test,
I know I have to play chess;
Because even the good guys
like to play games
when they're bored.

And the ones that say they love you more?
They're the ones
keeping track of the score.

Heart Gallery

This is not the museum of Me,
Anymore.
I've forgotten what my heart, mind and body
were for.
I just cry out in vain
and paint with my pain
And I'm racking my brain
Why do these all look the same?
My tears taste unfamiliar to me
salty like the Dead Sea
And the waves come crashing in angry
Because I don't know who I am, anymore.
I watch tears mix with the ink
As I'm buried at sea
Little pieces of me
Signed on every piece.
Stolen .
And now found aboard this Galley.
You wanted treasure
 But you found me.
I'm no longer gracefully placed
 in the place
where you lied to my FACE
That place
I gave my EVERYTHING for-

When I refused that day to stop walking the
plank you decided I'd instead hang…
On your wall
like I'm nothing at all
In your Gallery-
A Heart At War.

Once Upon A Time

Our 'Once Upon A Time ' exists only on paper
torn out and scattered across the floor.

You can hear the whispers from the pages..
Handwritten ghosts , "I love you more".

I never was a princess needing saving.
 Yet you showed up wearing armor at my
bedroom door.

 And now I see there never was a happy ending
you were just a dark knight, keeping score.

How could I ever believe in fairytales,
When I don't even love me anymore?

Paris

17

Once, you said you'd take me to Paris.

Now, I see you couldn't care less.

Why am I still lying on your bare chest?

Why do you still leave me breathless?

My heart beats so fast it's restless.

I can't believe you did this.

Since I've Been Dead

Hotel sheets are hearts that beat.
Two sets of bones, one body.
Your breath heavy on my shoulders.
It's a weight that I can't hold up.
Empty soul and spinning head.
You decided to love her instead.
You can't put back all the tears I've shed,
Your warm body
My cold bed
It's felt this way since I've been dead.

After

Inhale.
I let it go a little faster.
Got a new car
wanna crash it
Guess who I named it after?

After .
You gave me all this heartache
Don't wanna face my mistakes
But you fucked me up
For Christ's sake.

Before.
You slammed the door
in my face ,
Told me that I take up too much space
made up a war while my heart breaks
What the fuck am I fighting for?

After.
Now my life is a disaster
Running, don't know what I'm chasing after.

After.

What am I supposed to do after?

Magic tricks

Someone should have taught her, she's just
somebody's daughter, they should have fought
harder to guard her.

These demons that guard her and sit at her table ,
they break her and make her unable to love.

So she's breaking her back
Pulling tricks out of her hat
Wishing magic could make sense out of love
But once everyone disappears
All the spells she's cast turn into tears
Still she's expected to pull out a dove.

She's so used to the rabbits
Can't break her bad habits
Cuts herself into halves
And can't find her way back in this labyrinth.

Must be magic.
That her life feels so tragic
Happiness she can't have it.

She sees others that have it
And thinks...
It's all just a magic trick.

Crisis

Hitting all the rails
I'm in crisis
Here's a bullet
Please just bite this.
And my hair , I just pull it
Like I'm lifeless
I can't tell you why I'm like this
I knew that you were hell
since the first kiss
But I like this
Don't know where my mind is
I'm in crisis
Why am I like this?

Like You Failed Me

They say that some things
take a little longer
I wish I were a little stronger
I feel like I don't belong here.
Does that matter?
What if I don't like me after
I get what I'm chasing after?
Got my finger on the trigger
YOU dodged a bullet?
Fucking figures.
Dont know why I can't be happy
All these ghosts just keep on haunting
Demons crawling on the ceiling
I hate feeling.
Like a crazy train derailing
And I'm screaming please just help me
Always feeling like I'm failing.

Like you failed me.

Boneless Caviar

Can't you see my battle scars cut out of me in
pieces, shaped like paper hearts .
Once you made me feel like caviar.
Why did you push so fucking hard?
We had it all before the war....
But now all my wishes fall with dying stars.
I feel soulless
Like it's all just hopeless
Like I don't know what the word 'no' is.
I can't fill this
If I can't feel just
Where the hole is.
I'm boneless.
And you know this.

Printed in the USA
CPSIA information can be obtained
at www.ICGtesting.com
CBHW050458201024
15901CB00108B/1274